# MICHAEL JACKSON
## Instrumental Solos

Arranged by BILL GALLIFORD, ETHAN NEUBURG and TOD EDMONDSON

Produced by
Alfred Music Publishing Co., Inc.
P.O. Box 10003
Van Nuys, CA 91410-0003
alfred.com

ISBN-10: 0-7390-7800-3
ISBN-13: 978-0-7390-7800-6

# CONTENTS

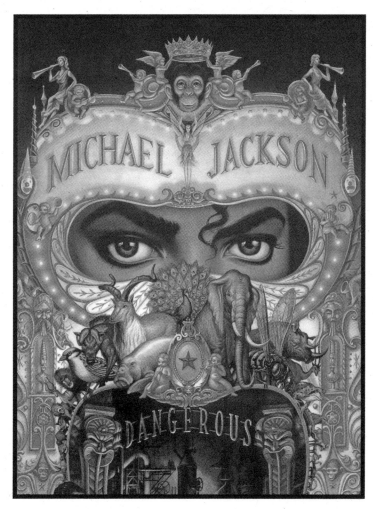

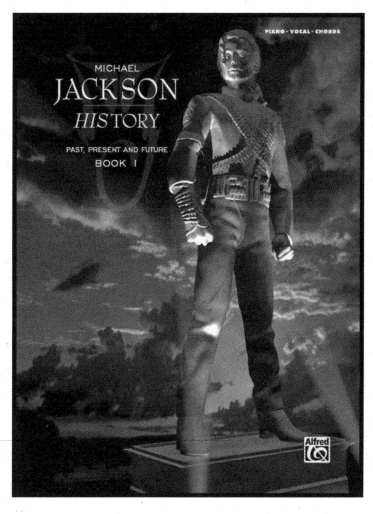

Track 2: Demo
Track 3: Play Along

# BEAT IT

Written and Composed by
MICHAEL JACKSON

**Moderately fast** ♩ = 138

Beat It - 2 - 1

# BILLIE JEAN

Track 4: Demo
Track 5: Play Along

Written and Composed by
MICHAEL JACKSON

Billie Jean - 2 - 1

# BLACK OR WHITE

Rap Lyrics Written by
**BILL BOTTRELL**

Written and Composed by
**MICHAEL JACKSON**

 Track 6: Demo
Track 7: Play Along

*(Spoken:) Protection for gangs, clubs, and nations,*     *causing grief in human relations.*

Black or White - 2 - 1

It's a turf war, on a global scale. I'd rather hear both sides of the tale.

You see, it's not about races, just places, faces. Where your blood comes from is where your space is.

I've seen the sharp get duller, I'm not going to spend my life being a color.

# DON'T STOP 'TIL YOU GET ENOUGH

Track 8: Demo
Track 9: Play Along

Written and Composed by
MICHAEL JACKSON

**Moderate dance tempo** ♩ = 112

Don't Stop 'til You Get Enough - 2 - 1

12

# HUMAN NATURE

Words and Music by
JOHN BETTIS and JEFF PORCARO

Track 10: Demo
Track 11: Play Along

Human Nature - 2 - 1

# I JUST CAN'T STOP LOVING YOU

**Track 12: Demo**
**Track 13: Play Along**

Written and Composed by
MICHAEL JACKSON

**Moderately** (♩ = 100) *Verse:*

I Just Can't Stop Loving You - 2 - 1

*Chorus:*

**37**

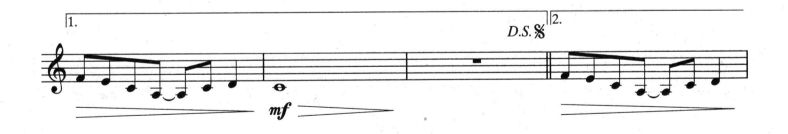

# THE WAY YOU MAKE ME FEEL

**Track 14: Demo**
**Track 15: Play Along**

Written and Composed by
MICHAEL JACKSON

The Way You Make Me Feel - 2 - 1

To Coda ⊕

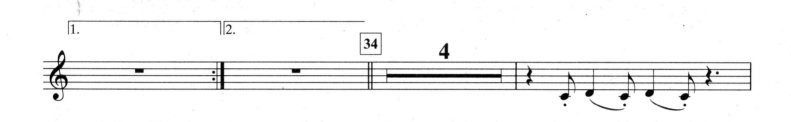

D.S. 𝄋 al Coda

⊕ Coda

# SHE'S OUT OF MY LIFE

**Track 16: Demo**
**Track 17: Play Along**

Words and Music by
TOM BAHLER

**Slowly, with expression (♩ = 72)**

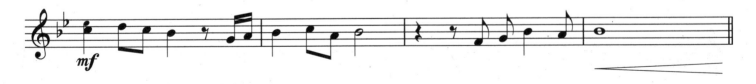

She's Out of My Life - 2 - 1

She's Out of My Life - 2 - 2

# WILL YOU BE THERE

Track 18: Demo
Track 19: Play Along

Written and Composed by
MICHAEL JACKSON

Moderate gospel feel (♩ = 80)

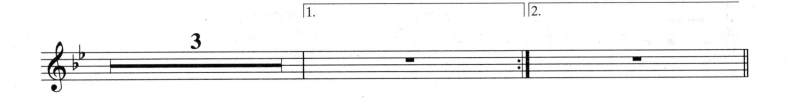

**22** *Bridge:*

Will You Be There - 2 - 1

# MAN IN THE MIRROR

Words and Music by
SIEDAH GARRETT and GLEN BALLARD

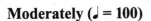

**Moderately (♩ = 100)**

Man in the Mirror - 2 - 1

# THRILLER

**Track 22: Demo**
**Track 23: Play Along**

Words and Music by
ROD TEMPERTON

**Moderate R&B rock** ♩ = 108

Thriller - 2 - 1

Track 24: Demo
Track 25: Play Along

# YOU ARE NOT ALONE

Words and Music by
R. KELLY

You Are Not Alone - 2 - 1

**Chorus:**

# PARTS OF THE HORN AND FINGERING CHART

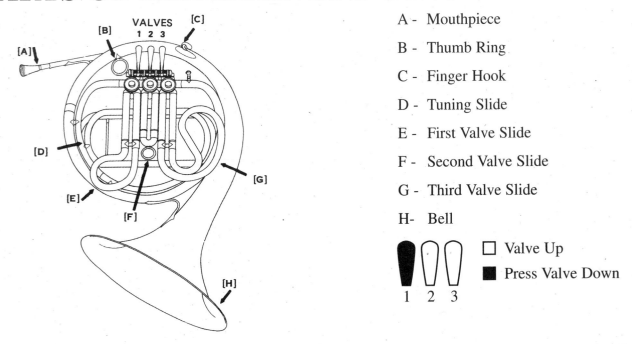

A - Mouthpiece

B - Thumb Ring

C - Finger Hook

D - Tuning Slide

E - First Valve Slide

F - Second Valve Slide

G - Third Valve Slide

H- Bell

☐ Valve Up

■ Press Valve Down

F Horns use the top fingerings. B♭ Horns use the bottom fingerings. F/B♭ Double Horns use the top fingerings without the thumb, or the bottom fingerings with the thumb. A good rule is to play notes from the second line G down on the F Horn, and from the second line G♯ up on the B♭ Horn.

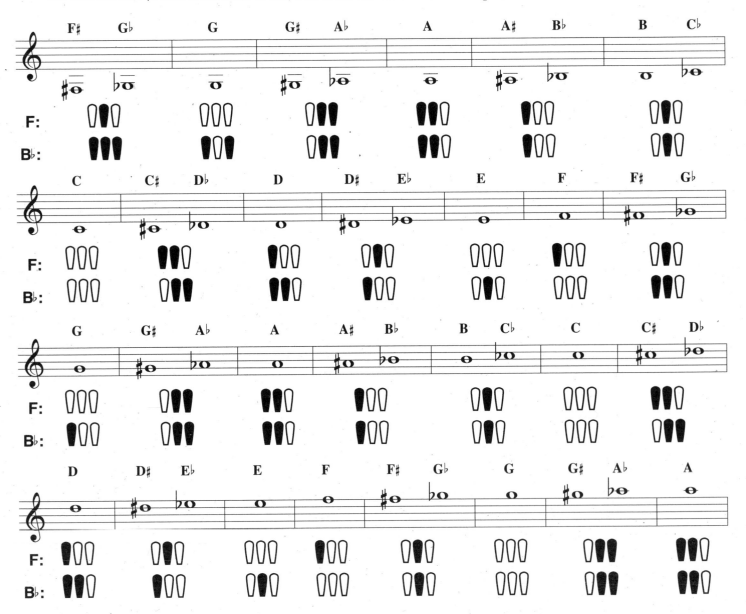